WATCHFULNESS

Peter O'Leary

SPUYTEN DUYVIL

ISBN 1-881471-73-X

Spuyten Duyvil
http://spuytenduyvil.net
1-800-886-5304

Acknowledgements

Some of these poems first appeared in *Poetry New York*, *LVNG*, *Nedge*, *Explosive*, and *Talisman*.

"Watchfulness" first appeared as *Backwoods Broadsides Chaplet Series* Number 21; "Ikons" as *tel let* 67; "Midas" as the fourth in the *pny / meb* pamphlet series. Gratitude to Sylvester Pollet, John Martone, and Tod Thilleman, who respectively published these.

Special thanks to Michael O'Leary, Devin Johnston, and Rebecca Houze, who attended to this book with their own forms of watchfulness.

for Ronald Johnson
my Mme Curie
"compression & radiation"   `

—in memoriam 1935-1998—

...gold
Shines like flaming fire at night...
—Pindar, Olympian i

Contents

I. IKONS

The gold coverage comes first: background, haloes, and so forth.

—Leonid Ouspensky, "Technique of Iconography"

<u>IKONS</u>

IKON

Gold flood entire air whole and
light elong body an ideal Lord

Cosmos

Gold, myrrh—soot
and smoke.
Women stoop, thrice
cross themselves

—image in ancient glow, kiss
the dark hand.

Alive!

SAINT-MAKER

Lord crowd his brow, rendered saints arrayed

a full material cosmos
a body in prayer bridges—

east & west
gesture & action—

in golden legend absent of shadow.
Of me
he is.

THE CRETAN STYLE

Fiery aureole
slender-fingered forms

recline in; spirate
angels suspend
in gold chorus;

wood block world
an oval veil of yolk.

PALAMITE

Gentle Greek Work

essence unseen
source & cause

yet energy range
regenerate in flesh

even now an endless well-
spring of sanctification.

HOLY NAMES

emanate around the Saint,
eliptic script an axis
hieratic heirs

eclipse light with gold along.
Cipher Saint(sparkling)hood.

Axios

Once sainted he
is fire-struck and
God-made, rhythm

of one law guide
hosts of gold and world—

irradiant luminary propped up,
beheld & held.

TREE OF LIFE

icon
scion

THE GOLDEN AGE

Honey won from light, thyme
& marigolds,

now amber sap &
saffron comb. Persephone orders out
Gods buzzing in
pollen pantaloons

to die stinging.

The Risen Lord garlanded
with a necklace of dessicated bees.

SUNDIAL

Name-laden man-
dala,

"this huge convex of
fire,"

increates an
Arch-chimic garden—

a Russian
miniaturist's monumental icon shield,
a polished Aztec calendar, or

Milton's solar gold—

where its style cuts
a shadow cast from spirit mirrors flow-
'ring in stars.

Eye

Ah lachrymose
Alchymyst

dares the slippery mercury
a storm dæmon bore bottled in
volatile lumen.

Bodies forth God's
abode in Greek gold, "the red blood
of silver,"

a sun in four winds.

Diviner's crystal exemplar,
a russet oval, coated in self-amalgam, is
his cooling water-vase, a looking-glass.

An Icon for Rob A. Davis

SUNBEAM

Spar turned oar
fans and threshes wheat in an
outland—:

fit the boom of God into the earth, bar
of a balance rimey with pilgrimage.

Alfredus Magnus, scholar—king,
brought across *columna lucis*
in his 9th C. tongue

as "a building post made from
a tree," and "sun"—.

Grip images light's logarithms
print patterns of in upper air radiant
with an ocular account of
wave & locus:

a *sunnebeam*.

GOLD

Cenobites mine the sky
for blood of yellow flowers, a powder
whose veins flush

like swallows through a dawn
they burn

in a crucible of tincture,
wood & egg turned

into a glimmering ash
of XPS.

THE HOUSE OF MY IKON

Its History
Two coastal holy
monasteries flank Stavorinikita
named for

St Nicolas

whose icon it houses;
pulled from the sea it bore
a big oyster on its fore-
head.

Oyster stuck off, a
lot of blood flowed from

the icon.

Patriarch Jeremiah II in its presence
in awe split
the shell: entreasured

one half among Monastery
relics, gave one half to Job
in Russia kept in
synodic vestry. The sea

sweeps
a wide view.

The Holy Church
Fire ruined
in 1538:

Jeremiah most reverent
acts—

rebuilt it a cenobite; enriched
now with votives, sacred treasures, holy

relics of Saints,

& books.

Sea-beaten cliff
In 1870 40 monks; 25
in 1903; and 4
today. An

aqueduct quarried
in 1666. All lying
eastward once burned—.

The Library
Tower the work of
the 11th Century.

Sacred Relics
i. Lower jaw
of St John the Baptist with
two grinders;

ii. Myrrh,
fragrant; iii. Relics
in bulky mix of

two myriads martyrs
of Diocletian's persecutions; iv.

Piece of left
hand of Agia Anna grandmother
of XPI; v. Skull

of holy martyr Phocas; vi.
XPI became his own symbol, an extended horizon;
vii. others.

Its Icons
Tree, temple, holy
mountain, inner
man a human harmony
divine;

shine
like tapers,
icon contact point,

worship
portable,

hand outfilling bodily
sight of Mt Tabor.

Who finds divine
energy generates

light in Gregory's

words, "for our part
we are certainly far from
knowing these things."

The Pantocrator of Christa
Mine:
climbed high city
hoar light toward

where gilt wood prevails.

Her John
the Precursor; her
Archangels;

her small XPI cosmos
now kept in my adoration.

Afire Patmos free,

her light its

atmosp
here

gold.

MIDAS

Streyght the powre
of making gold

for Ronald Johnson

King Midas' diamond mind
asking instant aurifex fired the world, & faulted.

Midas rises
from his throne in Turkey masked in light
hammered from its material component to resemble
the finest Mycenean foil:
Midas disguised as an Agamemnon of baubles, his
riches each wretched.

"Gold & silver we will tell them
they have from God; the diviner metal is within them,
and they have therefore no need of the dross which is current
among men, and ought not to pollute the divine
by any such earthly admixture;
for that metal has been the source of many unholy deeds,
but their own is
Undefiled."   [Plato, The Republic]

Orpheus was Midas' teacher;
without him the Mediterranean world is lost.
He ventured to Phrygia to play new modes for the oafish king
whose sin soaks the banks of *Pactole* to this day.
Upon the clods dense yellow the river
gutters with golden streams to swim;
where, once, bedlam howling out, *bluddy hands* cutting tunes,
frantic outrage reigned as women
to *Orphy* went and tore him limb from limb.

Songs drummed from his talisman's silver soul
dissolved foreign energies and drew them into their own.
Vatic Thracian thrashing Cicones spied, a tectonic crash
beheld, "See,
see, he is our contemptor!"
Orpheus percussed nervous songs

wreathing spears maenads hurled in leaves;
mad stones tossed took up Pythagorean orbits:
fractious Berecynthian clamor— flutes, cornets,
tympanies—& ululated
Bacchanals drowned *Orphy's* sound.
Ruddy stones are poet's blood. His scattered
members made a locus. His body
in sundry places Bacchus mourned.
His head & lyre Hebrus took. *A woundrous thing.*

[Metamorphoses xi:1-51]

A gift figured in guile divines
the grieving Twice-born Bacchus,
the voice lost who sang his mysteries, beheaded;
Orpheus' bobbling crown awash,
his livelesse toongue oh lord does speak.

Women oaks moan—*Suffring not this meeschief
unrevenged to be*, the Wine God
pinned his orgiasts' toes
with *writhen roote in ground*; they turned to trees.
A 'Prelude & Ground *à 5*' hums Byrd-like
the Phrygian Airs with catgut & plectre Orpheus
pulled on his viol, more dirgy
than Lydian modes whose somber orgies he'd taught Midas.
Reeds he'd practice on, a puerile Pan, have origins
in Asia Minor. They grow in swampy rushes where a flicker lighted
in grassy shadow taps on tin roofs a *wicka wicka wicka*: yellowhammers.

[Auduban's *Field Guide to the Birds
of North America,* Eastern Region]

Midas the hillbilly king
chicken-picken Orphic ballads on his dobro
daydreamed of winning the lotto and of moonshine.
Silenus, chief herald of Wine, was sauced; got lost on his ass.
For harboring Silenus Bacchus granted Midas a wish—
gold flowers, gold wall, gold cloth—
his daughter, his meat, his plate. He starved & thirsted.
Rejoycing in his harme he towcheth

every thing. A dish of worms & venomous insects
become ornaments: golden bugs & plated beetled bracelets.
Midas exhorted Bacchus: "Father God
have mercy on me for this ripe damnation."

Numen of Gods: might. The God spoke:
"Go to the magnum river near Sardis,
climb its declivity to the flume's source spuming fountains—
pleroma flowing out—
plunge body & head once—: make of your crime a similitude."
The king issued out succeeding waters: gold tincture & human water
                                            gushed & eased out.
Arms spanning head-waters, Pactolus burnished in sunlight,
Midas' spoils spill pools & currents with a radiant runoff—
Silts still glitter.
Semen & vein make fields hard & yellow—
Semolina & wheatstalk in Asia Minor to this day yield
golden harvests.

Once upon a time, Prospero's Orpheus armed with maps made from
acid-treated metal plates goes down to Hell for love but lost—
Maps scorched, their signatures remain copper lace & ash
he smelts & shapes into coils for wires
he will pluck with his teeth.
Say from his corpse Apollo the hurdy-gurdy player
made fiddlepegs with his long fingerbones
he wrapped with Orphic guitar strings.

Tmole the auncient
judge rids his ears of trees, keeps a garland of oaks on his hills
& listens: Pan plays rustic pipes &
the Sun-God halo'd in wicker wreath appears.
The head-dress essential for the ritual, he destroys at each
contest. Apollo sent his sister predator in search of shorebirds;
her hunting expeditions yield feathers for a new crown made up of
a fan-shaped diadem; he wears a feather visor covering
the upper part of the face, a high cylindrical crown
surrounding the head and made of rods surmounted by harpy-eagle

feathers,
and a wickerwork disc set with a bristling mass
of stalks stuck with feathers and down.
The whole head-dress is almost two metres high.

[Claude Lévi-Strauss, *Tristes Tropiques*]

He strings his gourd,
inlaid in Indian ivory, his pick a gull's wing-bone,
& frets a complete string music of galliards & pavanes,
some sung, some strummed, most bowed; rocks, trees, & streams
move nowhere, but breezes circle the mountain, bended rapid winds—
Tmolus has no doubts—Apollo wins. Midas opts for Pan—
What an Ass!

Leaving Boulder
the Colorado cuts gouges through the Rockies.
Prospectors shovel clumps from the hills and trolley
loads to slotted flues sluicing riverwater they rinse their dirt in.
We asked one, "Are you looking for gold?"
"Isn't everybody?" he said, a panhandler.
Imagine penitent Midas on Mt. Tmolus
performing forest austerities
where Pan handles reeds he's fluted & notched for fingerings.
Midas has asses' ears his barber can't keep secret.
Midas' lust for gold made him an ear
for Orpheus, for wishes, and for woodwinds.

II. LOOT

Every beloved object is the focus of a paradise
—Novalis

In gold the Age was sated, and Faith & right
sponsored empty retribution. Penal meting
& aberrations nor law nor words were *In brazen tables nayled up.*
They lived without vindicators—.
Not yet *hewen,* the *Pynetree*
pilgrim had not yet come down to the liquid air orbed
in shore, felled from *mountaines where it stood.*

Streames ran milk
streames ran wine
yellow honny flowde

But Lord Saturn into crepuscular *Lymbo*
was harrowed and errors reigned.
Silver proles marched in; Gold deteriorated.
And auncient Spring did Jove abridge.
Third came Brazen Ages. Horror prompted wars &
hard *yron* forged at the hands of the righteous
smote the darkness & the light at last.   [*Metamorphoses* 1:89-126]

Virga aurea facta est.

Byzantium,
"A Glittering Culture—"
their splendor of achievement was frescoes &
brilliant mosaics, exquisite ivory carvings, illuminated
manuscripts; churches phosphorescent with gold
where Holy Daniel prefiguring the resurrection raises hands
above Darius' fierce lions, tame as hunting dogs, & honors
the sanctuary of Hosios Loukos at Phocis aglow in honey
-colored light. The Byzantine Empire they called
the *œkumene,*
          "the universe."

Emperor Nicephoras Phocas in the 10th C. said of monks:
"The monks possess none of the evangelical virtues.
Instead, they horde huge buildings, horses, cattle, camels,
& livestock, their energies devoted only
to their own enrichment.
How the ecumenium moved since the lives of
Holy Men who in past centuries dwelt in Ægypt,
Palestine, Alexandria, & Cappodocia as coppery wasps
in the combs of their delicate ascesis,
in an immaterial existence more that of angels than men,
I know not."
[Philip Sherrard, *Byzantium*]

Goldfilled goldfield glorified:
American, Mexican, Indian all crowded
with hidden golcondas in their names.
These make up an illusive Monadnock once imagined
for instance as Men of Han aswim in wealth that
Jesuits trading in Italian, Portuguese, & Spanish would seek out
& convert. Turn their burial rites & unload graves of tributes.
Missionary, transhumant, gravedigging.

May 28, 1498, the King of Calicut wore green velvet,
a golden cup in his left hand two *palmas* wide. He spat husks
of herbs he chewed, grinning at their soothing effects,
his teeth & gums a menstrual
red. They called it *atambar*. Before him
a basin of gold a man might encircle with his arms
containing betel-nuts; silver jugs; a canopy of spun gold threads.
Vasco & Paulo da Gama moored in the harbor for days—
prepared a present for the King: *lambel*, scarlet hoods,
hats, a string of coral, a case of sugar, two casks of oil and two of honey.
Their Muslim interpreter scoffed: the poorest merchant
from Mecca or any other part of India gave more:
to make a fit profit, it must all be gold.
[*Roteiro* of Vasco da Gama]
The King of Calicut to the King of Portugal:
Vasco da Gama, a Gentleman of your household, came to my country,
whereat I was pleased.
My country is rich in cinnamon, cloves, ginger,

pepper, & precious stones. That which I ask of you
in exchange is gold,
silver, corals, and scarlet cloth.   [*Roteiro*]

The gold of the world laps an isthmus dubbed El Dorado
by seekers in heresies & curios, precious stone, converts, & conquests.
Hernan Cortez walks hand in hand with Montezuma through
Mexico City's aviaries confettied with species culled
Noah-like from the continent's furthest reaches. Bright finches
sharpen their beaks on honed-wood cages Cortez would soon torch,
setting the soul of the empire ablaze.
Montezuma explains the principle Aztec cities exact taxes
on all the produce in the kingdom & enumerates
the nature & variety of tributes:
cotton dresses, mantles of featherwork exquisitely stitched;
vases & plates of gold, gold dust, bands & bracelets; crystal,
gilded, & varnished jars & goblets; bells, paper, copper utensils;
grains, fruit, copal, amber,
cochineal, cacao, wild animals & birds;
timber, lime, mats, & c.

A calculus of riches,
the stones used in whose reckoning are gold-plated or obsidian
& clattering in the palms of Montezuma's accountants:
"20 chests of ground chocolate, likewise 2000 loaves of very white salt
refined in the shape of a mould for the consumption of the Lords of Mexico;
800 *xîcaras* out of which they drank chocolate;
a little vessel of small turquoise stones; 4000 loads of lime;
tiles of gold, of the size of an oyster, and as thick as the finger,
20 bags of gold dust of the finest quality;
a diadem of gold of a specified pattern;
20 lip-jewels of clear amber, ornamented with gold;
200 loads of chocolate; 100 pots or jars of liquid-amber;
8000 handfuls of rich scarlet feathers; 40 tiger skins"

[Wm. H. Prescott, *The Conquest of Mexico*]

Tenochtitlan, its "rude magnificence,"
was aglow with red porous amygdaloid, *tetzontli*,
quarried from the neighborhood, a light brittle stone

Spanish smiths and artisans admitted the Aztecs wrought
with amazing little difficulty into
crystal fountains embellished with porphyry and jasper
which from city centers "shed a grateful coolness
over the atmosphere."

[Diaz, *Hist. de la Conquista*]

Mexicans acquainted *gret marvayle* with minerals:
Silver, lead, & tin they drew from the mines of Tasco; copper
from the mountains of Zacotollan. Crude masses on the surface—:
Veins wrought in solid rock into which they opened extensive
galleries. Gold found on the surface gleaned from beds of rivers
cast into bars, or in the form of dust.
The use of iron, impregnating their soil, unknown to them.
Using a siliceous dust they cut basalt, porphyry, amethysts, &
emeralds, the hardest substances:
They fashioned these last into large, curious, & fantastic
forms, vessels of gold & silver carving them with their metallic chisels
in a very delicate manner.
"But especially,
they imitated very nicely the figures
of animals, and, what was extraordinary,
could mix the metals in such a manner that the feathers on the moveable wing
of a bird, or the scales of a most curious
fish, should be alternately of gold & silver."

[Wm. H. Prescott, *The Conquest of Mexico*]

Gold Rush shrug lodes from silver veins tapped
on frontiers of them hills—.
Boom-towns, harlots, & hooch in the hands of
miners & prospectors—
Arizona, Nevada, California, & the Yukon—
shovel-scrapes
carved devotional grottoes shaped to hold
what light earth's wealths gave off.
Fire light luminesced on
corn-cakes (1 portion corn-meal;
1 portion water; fried in hot skillet bacon-grease)

& coffee (chocked with chicory); after the meal,
smokes & the drizzle of a throaty tar.
On a cotton tick, pick axes, leather gloves & other
such riches struck.

An inward scintillescence
hoards the sun's lodestone.
Gold effuses even in gloom.
There's a free-silverite terror
of society without money where goldbugs
see more than enough to go around.
Gold like
cows or corn.
"It has been said that silver and gold have no intrinsic value;
this is not true. They are the only things used by Webster
in the copy of his dictionary which I have
to illustrate the meaning of the word
'intrinsic.'"

Miser silverites,
Midas goldbugs,
Magpies each.

"The American love of filthy lucre in the Gilded Age"
haloed Grover Cleveland when he reached for
John Haberle's meticulously painted five-dollar bill
on the library table in the White House. *O trompe l'oeil.*
                    [Walter Benn Michaels *The Gold Standard & the Logic of Late Capitalism*]

Herakleitos says Asses would rather have hay than gold.
From straw Rumplestilskin spun his metalled filament.

III. LUSTRATIONS

Sun crown worn new;
craved *arcanum arcanorum* in the meridian of
a solar genius' palm: illumination & rapture
at the feminine coiffure—.
Gold is "circulatory work of the sun."   [Michael Maier, 1598]

Osiris is lead & sulfur in
"The Dictionary of Goldmaking";   [Jung, *The Spirit Mercurius*]
The Nile, branching Tree of Life,
whose roots from several sources draw,
runs with milky quicksilver; it is vessels
of his severed body.
Vessel of Poimandres a uterus of spiritual renewal:
river font of shining water runs with Osiris, dismembered
God *par excellence.*   [Jung, *Visions of Zosimos*]

Four several-thousand years' cycles,
& the human family will be swept from the earth,
sun blotted from heavens giving
"a new aspect to the globe."
"They passed, at once, into the presence
of the Sun."   [Dante, *Paradiso*]

Songs & choral dances spun from filament.
Bright progress through heavens.
Singing birds of beautiful plumage.
"On the death of a person, his corpse was
dressed in the peculiar habiliments of his
tutelar deity.   [Wm. H. Prescott, *The Conquest of Mexico*]

Paper strewn as charms—the dark road he would take.
Gold the value of 3000 castellanos
drawn from his tomb if he were rich.
Priests would dazzle the imagination.
They would perceive in the vegetal or cosmic order a tremendous
shudder of meaning.

Sunlight sheds its luminism, a typical
epic of clear ice whose colors are three:
silver, emerald, & fawn.
America is the Harmonial ideal of "Solar Man"—
Light emanating from humans is a myriad spiritual
fuel for transformations, from love to song, desire
to lesson, conquest to lore. The world is known
in uniform gold.

The metal of the Sun is gold; its ruling Arch-
angel is Michael.
Of hypothetical Planets Midas is Sun
discovered by clairvoyant astronomers
in whose melothetic man Midas governs the heart
out of harmony with the Stellar music
and its Phrygian tones Eudoxos the Pythagorean conceived.
Moving Sun impinging on the paths of the planets
Fludds the welkin agilded.
"Music is faint
tradition of the angelic state."   [*Arkana Dictionary of Astrology*]

King Midas sings mild joy and holds his grail.
He changes it unavailed
from gold to gold.

II. HOLY TRINITY

"...their deep and lyric sense of the cosmos..."
  —John Meyendorf, "The Hesychast Tradition in Russia"

That low West that I've so often fed on, with a
sombre but intense crimson vestige smouldering
close to the horizon-line economical but
profound, and the western well of sky shading
upward from it through infinite shades of
transparent luminosity in darkness to deep blue
darkness overhead. It was purely American.
You never see that western sky anywhere else.
  —Wm to Henry James, 1904

WATCHFULNESS

Watchfulness is a way of embracing every virtue, every commandment. It is the heart's stillness and, when free from mental images, it is the guarding of the intellect.

—St Hesychios the Priest, 8th or 9th c.

Agios o Theos

Divine isle evince
illumination

in Bronze Sea Blue in-
apprehensible &
rich with radiance dolphins
sport in the sea of,

combed with coral
volcanoes, "hard to be uttered" (HEB. 5:11). From Moni Ioannis
Theologos Turkey kneels into the water
eastward and Xoros the hushed
high town in the apron of St John
hums above noon silver like pine wax
buffing the air on Patmos.

No man
is safe from changing

the bright, the sun,
and, "so I speak" (JOHN 12:58)

an anemnesis of Ægean
theophanies spied in Louis Sullivan's
numinous carpentry

taught from olive-cradle
archipelago to Constantinople
and by envoy to Kiev newly bathed
in gold through a millennium to
Ukrainian Village, Chicago, Illinois
on the corner of Haddon & Leavitt, where in 1899 on seeing half-laid plans,
the antique Holy Spirit iridesced
& smote its new lumen through American fingers & eyes.

Hesychia

The Lord is Odysseus in our Body
the Stars glutted with miracles; his vessel is Holy
Trinity; I am his companion

"seeing the churches of God bright
with the sacred."

Odysseus is sundered
for leaving the Mediterranean. I float it
on a little Phoenician raft.

Turquoise air an intoning voice announces
My Soterion restored in
holy icons splendors fire
three-fold as
"mystery divine knowledge"

& magnify.

Relics flow with holy oil
clerics loft in censed processions to
reenact tumult, temple, holy mountain:

a living man happening,

pure name ripe
& exalted in luminous spires

or sacramental decorations worked from
terrible light; church stucco is
stellated with its maker's palmistry.

Words are wrought & cast on

a deep cobalt flood of
stars

Avernal night ensues above.

At 9:30am, Sundays, the Divine Liturgy
begins.

Θ

Paul, deranged by the Lord,
first fled to Arabia:

What in the Lord's Word renders
fright?

Panagia at Apeiranthous
holds holy form
as Holy Trinity does
in chiliastic light—:

yet is it one?

Louis Sullivan
made his church alone
with books.

Did he ever see
Russian plains or
the white tiny huts of God
dark within

clustered like nests
on every outcrop in Hellas?
Was his Ægean imagined from the Protean

shifts in the color of Lake Michigan from
day to day? Was Cyrillic the samples of an apocalyptic
entomology in his eyes? Was Kiev the kernel
of the seed of New Byzantium?

Constantine & his older brother Methodius,
Saints of an earlier world,
far from Thessalonica tamed the barbarian language,
breaking the Slavonic sounds and salving them with a Greek tongue.
Sullivan made of the Ukraine a Chicago
style: eaves decorated like downtown; the doorframe
adorned with the lacework of a department store.

Θ

Illumination
of Naxian marble

in oratories before
oratories

before
the cleft rite:

light from amber
tapers casts up the crack'd fresco
XPC rifts all-ruling.

His robes of stars.
Hands still & held—:
His Eyes

alight
the musty catacomb:
dark hub

infolds an ark of space
under the dome carried on
pendentives over a square—:

incrustation
with marble, with clay,
but less gold, real or
paint, among the islands.

Wasps'-paper in concentric
mounds piles holy
nests of worship paths through sage-grass chart
with gravities these air
thrum with.

Lemon trees & thyme
dry in the high light
of Asia Minor,

a terrible pool of sun
a hive cools in

assembled by ages'
hymenopteran
architects

in some respects
Cycladic, early-worldly with inner
limestone-light

whose hue is
sea blue.

Nipsis

Desert firmament
watchful patterned energy

blooms in communion radiant above,
heart like a full moon,

Word a stone
St Hesychios the Priest kept in his mouth
for three years

to learn silence
Sinai protrudes toward,

show prayer gravities cloven
by star-like intellections
illuminated by saints

decorating cells,
white-washed chapels
icons aflow in gold glorify,

& cathedral
main domes

Louis Sullivan, ad-
ore-
ing & imagining, en-
visioned not as dense bodies

but as lightning spread through
hair-line lacquered fractures
of force on a ceiling of

cerulean & celestial

Caritas of exquisite
stars arisen in

skies of ice whose resplendent
rites, untiring, unite.

LUX HOMINUM

The name of man is a homonym
for birds of passage

The name of man is as impossible to find
as a solarheaded sphinx

or cymbals of lunar tinsel lying still
with the winds.

I have seen a spirited dog
destroying both wolves & sheep—

Your gloriole is lovely & awful
like conversion, like gold air,
like the word "cripple."

The name of man
would be turgid were it not that

bees classify luminosity in terms of
weight, darkness being heavy & brightness light

& that saracen mathematicians made of stars
an abacus, an algebra & made of the night sky
a book.

Holding the mirror of mind firmly
toward God, we will be illumined as pure glass
by divine fire.

The sun in your eyes
is Light; Light is
azure morning bells.

LUMINOUS GREAT MASS

Holy Trinity Airship
billows a

chrys-
elephantine
cave Louis Sullivan, Arch-
itect, lord master,
conceived of
in the hollow of power.

He swells.
I am his balloonist
balancing an azimuth

as earth-apse I
orbit, robed in
hot gas & leather

fastened by a yolk-stalk
of gravity to gold-
end onions nozzling heavens

whose suns are stomachs
with churches in their navels.

Each we are priests
as aeronauts at the vestibules,
& enter the cavity:

space, self, organ; celest-

ial nave
bellies

stars sailors name saints
and adore—

their egress is bitter
weeping, their praise pure
Russian form:

a cathedral,
my inner orrery.

TRANSFIGURED LIGHT

Barking dogs
floriate an aura—:
a Holy Ardor irradiates
most densely in a speculum.

Is it animated from the movements of stars?

is it a hymn, an organloft carved from marble, men intoning *cantus
        firmus*, Gregorian notations they hold in their hands?

a similitude of monks?

is it an inner laceration?

is it a cyclamen? a cataclysmic engraving of Odysseus at sea's edge?
        a halcyon cycle his soul's reborn in?

Blake immersed copper plates
in acid vats he'd examine the bubblings of
for spiritual courses reflected.

Is it an interpretation as false as Averroes' numerical Aristotle is salvific?
        as a sapphire is an appearance of blue? as Arabic glosses angelic
        epistolaries?

is it a feeling-toned idea thoroughly archaic in character?

A Θ marks a body's
horizontal passage through time, circumscribes it
with the beginning of the name of God.

Gives the Lord
a raiment of graphemes. An icon
comprised of an alphabet.

Is it Peter?

is it James? is it John brother of James?

is xpc a constellation in Cyrillic? a consequence? florid & hovering in
      gold?

Dante saw the cosmos as three auditoriums:
one going down-to; one going up-to; and one going
out-to a center,

petals enheavened in an amphitheater.

Is it a criminal? Ulysses sundered at exceeding the Middle-Sea beholding
      Columbus on Cuba lifts his hackles & growls.

What am I after really? What is my secret intention?

Is it heartbreak as in Gregory's giving up of the contemplative life?

is it the repetition of prayers, the delicate application of egg tempera, the
      aging & the miraculous restoration of icons, the windows into
      glorification?

is the unconscious world of images behaving as an object? is it the
      illumination at the sight of the Grail, which is a religious
      movement rarefied by photosynthesis, or a narrative of rites Celts
      recite in spelt occlusions? is it Parzival pierced the veil?

"is it always a few who reach the edge of the world, where its mirror-
      image begins?"

is it dæmonic?

Adam Kadmon beholds
his feet, shattered vessels tiptoeing
the *primum mobile*,

his footsteps drumming a surface
quaking with broken husks of clay once
the bright teeth of Seraphim.

Is it aviary or virid? or a calico sparrowhawk in Chicago winter
        entaloning a crucifix?

is it a communion of angels? is it the Areopagite, articulate of celestial
        hierarchies?

is it how winter feels from the distance of fall?

is it lustrous as an optical Doppler whose song is played on bow-
        harps or musical saws in its source's receding?

is it St Bernard of Clairvaux, *doctor mellifluous*, is it St John Chrysostom
        of the Golden Tongue? is it impressive of Serbian? is it beheld?

is it a tympanum, a laud, robed in white, a sensorium?

is it a tychism of luster fused through its artifice as in the tides among the
        Dodecanese receding, as in Sullivan's fresco-work on midwestern
        banks?

is it dynamic of clouds? a tychonic compression of the solar azimuth?

is it Diodocus of Photiki saying, "it is right always to wait, with a faith
        energized by love, for the illumination which will enable us to
        speak"?

is to dwell to die well?

is it intoxication of light? is it total light?

is it Symeon the New Theologian?

The way cloven by crystal makes
from thoughtfulness a floral outline; makes
a variation of sunlight.

Tongues purl around Slavonic tones.

Darkness is a glorious name caught in a throat.

Darkness is incantatory.

Sullivan is a wizard, a heretic, a cenobitic builder, a Noah, a nodule of
      clustered fires.

Light is ore

abhorred

hoar.

An America Sullivan Little Knew

In an Aleutian
Outland

Sts Peter & Paul
The Apostles, Chapel—

A Russian Cross & Russian
domes like those Sullivan emulated
in Chicago; but these are

one century older
& made of

cedar &
paint. Iron bells

hung from an eaves
crossbeam, skirted in

snow & a thousand-years'
irradiance. Skirted in a prostration
of archipelagos.

Russians on seeing Holy Trinity
think it "weird."

Poetic Light As Invisible Fire

> The divine light, being given in mystical experience, surpasses at the
> same time both sense and intellect. It is immaterial and is not appre-
> hended by the senses; that is why St Symeon the New Theologian while
> affirming its visibility yet calls it "invisible fire."
> —Vladimir Lossky,
> *The Mystical Theology of the Eastern Church*

In seeing, light fails; it harbors densities & terrible darknesses. Poetic
light, which is not the light of seeing, is also not the province of divine
revelation—: that is divine light. Poetic light is not a worldly light of
hearth—warm, nurturing, to be surrounded by. Poetic light is
transfigurative. This is not to say mediative: in no way does poetic light
shuttle back & forth between heaven & earth; divine & hearth. Poetic
light transfigures; poetic light is transfiguration. It is the light that exalts,
glorifies, illumines, idealizes, irradiates. Poetic light is invisible fire,
surpassing both sense & intellect. Poetic light penetrates even the *sinus*
of God. Inward light of increate grace, it is resplendent, like XPC on the
mount of Transfiguration:

And after six days Jesus taketh Peter, James, and John his brother, and
bringeth them up into an high mountain apart,
And was transfigured before them; and his face did shine as the sun, and
his raiment was white as the light.
(MATT 17: 1—2)

St Mark describes: "And his raiment became shining, exceeding white as
snow; so as no fuller on earth can white them." (7:2)

And St Luke: "And as he prayed, the fashion of his countenance was
altered and his raiment *was* white *and* glistening." (9:29)

Not surprisingly, perhaps, St John's gospel records no description of the
Transfiguration: as gospel it is entirely turned toward light, all
Transfiguring, inapprehensible: in ipso vita erat et vita erat lux hominum
et lux in tenebris lucet et tenebrae eam non comprehenderunt.

Moses & Elijah, both of whom spoke to God through fire, appear flanking ic xc. The disciples fall to their knees, enthused. They promise to build shrines to all three: Moses, Elijah, & ic xc. A Voice singles out His Son: the prophets vanish from the light.

The Transfiguration is one of the primary New Testament sites for Christian mystical contemplation (St Paul's elevation into the Third Heaven (2 COR 12) is the other). The Transfiguration is especially important to the mystical theology of the Eastern church; indeed, it is a centrality from which much Orthodox faith & practice are engaged in & defended. Mt Tabor is Holy Mountain; spiritual Sinai; heavenly axis. Without the scene of the Transfiguration, *hesychasm*, the praxis of repetitive mystical prayer (the famous "Jesus Prayer" or "Prayer of the Heart," names owing to the habit of repeating the name ic xc toward experiencing its luminous presence, kundalini-like, starting from the heart & pluming its holy torrents up through the body) would be empty muttering. A hesychast prays toward seeing xpc glorified, alight; toward seeing Transfigured light, invisible fire—: not an earthly light nor a divine light but nonetheless "divine," that is, *holy*. Holy how? Holy in being suffused with the energy of God. Divine light, distinct from Transfigured light, is entirely of the essence of God: unknown & unknowable to any woman or man.

Transfigured light, replete with the "rush (εξαλμα) of God," in the words of St Gregory Nazianzen, communicates *itself*, flows with force. Vladimir Lossky explains: "for the energies are not effects of the divine cause, as creatures are; they are not created, formed *ex nihilo*, but flow eternally from one essence to the Trinity. They are the outpourings of the divine nature which cannot set bounds to itself, for God is more than essence. The energies might be described as that mode of existence of the Trinity which is outside of its inaccessible essence. God thus exists both in His essence and outside His essence. Palamas says, referring back to St Cyril of Alexandria, that, 'creation is the task of energy; it is for nature to beget.'"

The poet stands in the umbrage of invisible fire, salamandrine refiner of "coalescent holocausts," hammering energy into syllables resplendent with the work of making.

Divine light of revelation recedes like a church tympanum to leave itself unknown by an absence; world light nourishes the heat I use to live, to cook, to rest—. Transfigured light is inherent composition in which we transform & are transformed. In the regenerate lordly rush of poetic light, we slip into a photic stream unbounded in time & space imperceptible to the senses but seen by the bodily eyes, in whose watchfulness we pass from flesh to Spirit: *spirit* as in psychic force; *spirit* as in active reverberance; *spirit* as in speaking again as the LORD once spoke. Light symbolism becomes name symbolism in our making of poems, writing them & receiving them. St John Climacus wrote: "The word of love is known to the angels and even to them only according to the energy of their illumination." Our spiritual body is stylus for poetic light to carve radiant glyphs on worldly tablets, slabs of pumice, tempering them in invisible fire, whose flames lick up into furnaces of divine light, stoked with an abhorrent fuel of stars. St Gregory Palamas is succinct: "He who participates in the divine energy, himself becomes, to some extent, light; he is united to the light, and by that he sees in full awareness all that remains hidden to those who have not this grace; thus he transcends not only the bodily senses, but also all that can be known by the intellect... for the pure in heart see God... who, being Light, dwells in them and reveals Himself to those who love Him, to His beloved."

I stoop before the body of poetic light, whose dazzle flows up from radical, deep-buried *logia* ored along massive rooted veins drawn into an aura of circulation, into luminous aortal gutterings, condensed at last into a fist hammering darkness shattered into a scintillant cuneiform of sparks, attentively ciphered into girandoles & concealments by watchful eyes.

MYSTIC PRAYER TO THE HOLY SPIRIT

St Symeon the New Theologian

Come, True Light.
Come, life eternal.
Come, hidden mystery.
Come, treasure without name.
Come, ineffable way. Come, body shaped of stars inconceivable. Come, endless felicity.
Come, ritual lustrations.
Come, light without Western horizon.
Come, flawless waiting of all who strive to be saved. Come, reveille for the sleepers. Come, resurrection of the dead. Come o Power Who shapes & reshapes & transforms in the energy of Your sole will.
Come o Invisible beheld but not held utterly beyond the tactile radius of hands and their shapings.
Come You Who dwell unmoving & Who at each moment propel Your total whole toward Your origin exploding, & Who come to us, sleeping in hells, o You shivering above all firmaments & all mornings.
Come o Name everywhere ceaselessly prayed & beloved of whose knowing we are absolutely forbidden to voice. Come, joy eternal.
Come, corona unwithering, solar hierophany.
Come royal purple of the Great King our Lord.
Come, crystalline sash constellated of jewels. Come slippered footstep quiet as forgetting. Come purple mantle.
Come You Who desired & desire my miserable soul.
Come, You the One, sole artificer of my solitude & its simulacrum, Your bosom of stars as prayer on my lips.
Come You who separate me from all & render this world solitary.
Come You becoming Yourself in my desire Who made me to desire You, You the illustrious specialist of the Absolute, inaccessible & expanding.
Come my asperance & my life. Come salve of my sore soul.
Come my joy, my glory, my energy compressed into a lavender autumn aster fraying, delights without end.
Come bright poetic torsion.
Come, light made of ash.

I give you thanks for having become one in spirit with me without
confusion, without mutation, without transformation,
You the Lord above all & for having become my total whole,
nourishment inexpressible & perfectly free,
Who overboiling endlessly is Creation, ebullient over the levees of my
soul & guttering back up to the source of my heart,
dazzling vestment consuming demons,
purification christening me in imperishable & holy tears You wrench
from those You flood.
I give You thanks for having become in me light without West,
sun never going down;
for You have nowhere to hide, no Hades to course through,
You Who emplenish the universe with Your Glory!
no, You hide Yourself to noone ever but it's we who always hide from You
refusing to go to You;
where then were You hiding, You Who find Your repose nowhere?
Why were You hiding, You Who receive, behold, & become each one
soul, You Who repel no soul?
Come then, o Master,
bivouac in me today; build up Your house & dwell continually,
inseparably, until the end times, in me, Your slave, o great good;
& at my departure from this world & after my departure,
that I find myself in You, o great good, & reign with You,
Lord above all.
Dwell, o Master, & do not leave me alone where enemies
& diabolical brigands supervene,
those foul lopers always crawling on their bellies to devour my soul
find You the Lamb in my fold,
genuine & ancient,
borne of chthonian epiphanies & golden, & hackles drawn in full pounce
they are caught, snared, powerless against one in seeing You,
You more mighty than all, enhomed in the interior, in the center of the
house of my poor soul.
Yes, Master,
You stand me before the face of Your Glory;
likewise, guard my inward body, upright always, unshakable,
in your dwelling in me:
that in seeing You perpetually, me, the dead, I live;

that in possessing You, I the poor one, I am always rich & rich beyond all
kings;
that in eating You & in drinking You,
in clothing myself in each instant in You, I go from delight to delight
a hummingbird
drawing nectar inexpressibly good from inverted flowers of your light:
for it's You Who are all good & all glory & all delight
& it's in You appear Glory, Holiness, consubstantial & living Trinity, You
Who venerates, Who confesses, Who adores & Who serves
in the Father, the Son, & the Holy Spirit all beliefs
per omnia sæcula sæculorum. Amen.

III. JERUSALEM

PS 47 *Magnus Dominus, et laudibus; in civitate Dei nostri, in monte sancto ejus*

Great is the Lord, and exceedingly to be praised; in the city of our God, in his holy mountain

IERVSALEM POSTCARDS

& brought me in visions
of God to Jerusalem
      —Ezekiel

Jerusalem Uprooter
unnerves destroyer terror—

light hallows a far-reach; photism fuels
Sarcophagous kiosk in the deep of Holy Sepulcher—

life-force infused.

Antependium of haze makes linen of dawn,
hidden city behind.
Its collosal roots.

ONE

Antique echo
the quaternity emplenishes

prayer-times. A rancid nacre runs through
marble gutters.

Armenian evening &
the fervors of boys at the theriomorph:
The Lord as King of Birds.

TWO

Messiah & Prophet

African tongues lapse diphthongs:
shibboleth is sibillant
Issa,

prophetic in his raiment;
brightness falls from the air onto the Navel
of the World—Rock

domed by Muslim algebrists in
great bliss uplifts hagiological legends
from doom: the Golden Dome

mathematically proportioned &
rhythmically perfect.

THREE

Edicule beneath dome
ablaze in Holy Sepulcher—

ambulatories plait numeric
serpents

fashioned from fractured *Nazarene* mosaics,
plunder of Allah,

in the Dome of the Rock.

A small reliquary
narrow & towering
above the Rock
holds hairs from
Muhammed's beard.

FOUR

Via Dolorosa

    Arch of pigeons
     span iconographers'
calendrical devotions muted through gold an
arc hoop reigns
over;
   hovers,
     solemn & Ethiopian.

FIVE

"My book is the sign I bear."

Jinn jostled Muhammed eager to embrace Islam—
intelligent creatures of Air & Fire.

Lassitude & error.
The Prophet's doubts.

Jews loathing Jesus turned Muhammed's face
from Jerusalem to Mecca.

Pilgrimage inconsiderable,
The Prophet's muezzin mounted the roof of Arabia
& called Muslims to prayer.

SIX

In sickness the Qur'an is the Muslim's
standby. Friends & relatives will enter
the sick-chamber & recite the Fatiha & the Throne verse.
Some people never leave their homes
without having a small copy of the Qur'an on their
person.

The faithful sometimes in rapt silence.
He is the Hearing, the Knowing.

A binding force
whose Semitic form
of mantic oracular utterance

the city chatters with.

SEVEN

78

Descent of the Holy Fire
candesces rebirth; a
hemisphairon
where desolation of the Lord is commemorated:
    hollow & granite.

EIGHT

Root of the Grail

Radish-shaped astronomy lodges the moment—
Its myth birthed in the city:

napiform & revered by Muscovites
as sky-radicals on orthodox spires.

The bowl of the Grail is bulbed—
its sanguinous roots through Jerusalem
dangle ruddy & vericose—.

NINE

A Book of Roots
would show line drawings of David
executed with psalmic paraphrases;

would begin with Jeremiah's tomb;

would be imaginatively recreated by the Prophets
even were it destroyed;

would have the soapy burnish
of Jerusalem stone;

would render parables whose Hebrew
would perplex even
the most flamboyant epigrapher;

would mention the bottom of the world
is a sea confounded with metals.

TEN

Jerusalem ruined
—its cyclopian rind harrowed, Tabor afar
loses light to niveous dust
I cannot breathe—awful city

rises through a suburb of ashes & hysterical
Chinese landscapes

in Jeremiad strophes I count out in loss.
New Jerusalem I build
in solitude;

an *aurifrigeum* embroidered with birds
decorates the monstrance
— "an image of the sun raised on a pedestal"—

burning above the sacristy
"a golden conflagration" of the solar logos.

Armenian clerics wash their foreheads,
snuff wax, kneel.

The city is prayer.
It gates me.

ELEVEN

EPHPHATHA

...in the figural system the interpretation is always sought from above; events are considered not in their unbroken relation to one another, but torn apart, individually, each in relation to something other that is promised and not yet present.

—Erich Auerbach "Figura"

In illo tempore:

At that time: Jesus going out of the coasts of Tyre, came by Sidon to the sea of Galilee, through the midst of the coasts of Decapolis. And they bring to him one deaf and dumb, and they besought him that he would lay his hand upon him. And taking him from the multitude apart, he put his finger into his tongue; and looking up to heaven, he groaned, and said to him: Ephpheta, which is: Be thou opened; and immediately his ears were opened, and the string of his tongue was loosed, and he spoke right. And he charged them, that they should tell no man; but the more he charged them so much the more a great deal did they publish it; and so much the more did they wonder, saying: He hath done all things well; he hath made both the deaf to hear, and the dumb to speak.

Sequentia sancti Evangelli secundum Marcum 7:31-37

Itinerant from Tyre to Sidon
circuitously through the Ten-Towns—:
deaf-mute deprecating at his hands. Apprehension.
XPC's digits swabbed his auricles

lingual adhesions glistening—:
he sighed & looked to skies & said it: *Ephphatha*.
It means: "be opened."

As of a loquacious solution freed through an aperture,
the words flowed rightly from the deaf-mute's tongue.
He spoke & he heard himself & ignored the admonitions
of the Lord.

all that is formed, all that is spoken
emerges from one name
                    —*Sefer Yetsirah*

A ngel of God—midrashists call Him God—
pulled his digits from his mouth & inserted them
in Jacob's ears—:
He cleaved Jacob's drums & probed seraphic carpels
into his sinuses where they throbbed.
He spoke to him: Speak your name.
Jacob tried: "Iakov." It came out: "Israel."
Jacob said to the Angel of God: "Ephphatha," *quod est*, "Speak your own name."
Jerking his hip, the Angel of God hobbled him there & departed.

In this *zohar* dwells the one who dwells.
It provides a name for the one who is concealed
and totally unknown.
It is called the Voice of Jacob.
—*Zohar*

Jacob's struggle with the demonic, his prevailing
over Lilit and Sama'el, clear the way for his ascent
to *Tif 'erat*, the *sefirah* of wholeness and balance.
Having attained perfection, he receives a new
name: Israel, "for you have struggled with
Superhuman and with human beings, and you
have prevailed" (Gen 32:29).
—Daniel C. Matt, "Notes," *Zohar*

Thus [the Lord] appeared to each of the holy
fathers, exactly as he wished and as it seemed
helpful to them. In one manner he appeared to
Abraham, in another to Isaac, in another to Jacob,
in another to Noah, Daniel, David, Solomon,
Isaiah, and to each of the holy prophets.
—Pseudo-Macarius (Syrian monk of the 4th c.)
"The 50 Spiritual Homilies"

The names Jacob and Israel refer respectively to
the ascetically active and to the contemplative
intellect which through ascetic labour and with
God's help overcomes the passions and through
contemplation sees God, so far as is possible.
—St Gregory of Sinai (1265—1346)
"On Stillness: 15 Texts"

Jabbok adumbrates Jordan—:
shadow of night will show morning sun,
salubrious Gallilean breezes—:
flight & exile prefigure healing, arisen lordly firmament.
Jacob's naming I make the suspiring of XPC.

Possible Origins Of Ephphatha

A Greek transliteration from the Aramaic
  'ethpatah, the causative of phatah, "to open."
A Greek transliteration from the Hebrew.
St Mark has assimilated the pronunciation of the Aramaic, part of
  the authentic speech of Jesus.
Like an Ephraimite hissing "shibboleth," a Samaritan enunciating
  the Hebrew "be opened" would say it, "affeta."
Genesis 49:1 has effata in the Palestinian pentateuchal Targum.
ephphatha: exists in the Babylonian Talmud;
                            absent in Jerusalem Talmud;
                            absent in Midrashim.
There is the symbolic gesture of spittle; spittle's role in early
  Roman baptismal rites.
"Be thou opened."

Also: the use of foreign phrases was characteristic of stories of
  wonder-workers; quod est: "hocus pocus."
This last is rejected by most scholars.

He sighs & looks up; or,
He groans & looks up—:

Star-Soul in outer manifestation
xpc sighs in his recognition of—:

the emanator relumined the mass of darkness with a ray of light
withdrawn at first, then hidden in text, spelt:
"*ephphath*a."

Thus Jephthah:
"for I have *opened* my mouth unto the LORD & I cannot
go back." (JUDGES 11:35)

ephphatha

monologic chautauqua
gospeleer pupil attends solely—:

concealment heard & preserved

Bethlehem harbors a silver star Greeks wrought their altar above.
They lord over this nativity carefully.
They've hung censers in hundreds. They sway
like aluminum seraphim in the air,
pendant chains lost in attic gloam.

Contiguous Franciscans attend catacombs burrowed under
their altar. Here St Jerome ensconced in a colon of buttery Jerusalem
stone exchanged the Word's phosphorescence for vulgar unguent.
Coming to a word that means "open up" he found
a sounded blackness he kept.
In opening up Greek, he closed it, mustering only: "eppheta"—:
he wrote it "adapirire."

Advaitic reader,
I write "Prefiguration" & watch it
spelled-out "Ephphatha." To Scripture, I say "ephphatha"
& feel Its letters tug on my tongue & bind it:
on one side my tongue; on the other the Word; between it, a
          Chinese finger puzzle.

XPC jammed fingers rheumy with mucous in the deaf-mute's ears.
XPC groped the deaf-mute's *lingua*, rubbed its nether-buds
with His blisters.
XPC imagined the deaf-mute speaking His name.
XPC winced; eyes pinched shut by cataracts of light.
XPC spoke: "Speak my name," *quod est*: "ephphatha."
The deaf-mute gagging heard "Emmanuel" slip out "Angel of God."
He felt the sinews ripping then as xpc dislocated his hip.
Known thereafter by his limping.
And thereafter by his lisp.

BLINDSIGHT

The Monastery of St. Catherine is an Orthodox monastical center with a continuous life since the 6th century. It has stood for 1400 years in the heart of the Sinai Desert, and preserved its special character since its erection in the era of Justinian (527-565 AD). Muhammed the founder of Islam, Arab caliphs, Turkish sultans, and Napoleon all took the Monastery under their protection, thereby preserving it from pillage: it has never in its long history been conquered, damaged or destroyed, and has through the ages kept its image as a sacred Biblical site, where the symbolic meaning of the events of the Old Testament is illuminated and interpreted in the worship of the Lord Jesus Christ and the Virgin Mary.

—Dr. Evengelos Papaioannou

In the Man of Light, the world transcended bears the gift of stars.

In Sinai, I made up through the mountain where massive night leaves
massive gloss shivering with syllables—

In the Man of Light, this is the light shown the first Adam:

>"with it he saw from one end of the world
>to the other."

In the Man of Light, this is the light hidden away so we would not make
use of it.

In the Man of Light, the Blessed Holy One gave the light to Moses—

the Blessed Holy One gave the light to Elijah—

in the Man of Light, they wielded dazzle their whole lives long.

The Blessed Holy One gave the light to Sinai, to Desert Fathers, to
Muhammed, to Sufis.

Its nimbus chimed. Tinntinnabular. Abuzz.

In climbing up, I palmed a Word dusted with pollen I put in my mouth.
It flowered there when I spoke it.

An Aster. A Carnation.
Holy Icons inscribed with Holy Names spangle voices: *Agios Moise*; *Agios
Elias*; *Aikaterina*; IC XPC.

As "chi" & "rho" make Roman letters X & P; & as "sigma" rendered in
Byzantine crescent makes "C";
so XPC is the name of the Lord; of man; of Man of Light invoked

as unutterable
as Constantinopolitan Christogram marking chasubles, manuscripts,
       icons, a namelessness
as *hapax legomenon*
as word appearing only once in the ancient text, with no other reference
       but itself:

> "Deep within the spark gushed a flow, the
> concealed within the concealed."

In the lambent torrent of primordial creation

> "The fire had a radiance & lightning
> issued from the fire."

Sunrise gleamed like beryl.

In the Man of Light, I know it, too;

> "be silent."

In scintillant pinpoints the light that guides me shines in full noon—: I
have seen it flashing. It is a map scratched out

in lightning cartography. It illustrates
a lucid earth on the palm of the hand of the Man of Light.

I am his Henry Hudson; He is my New World. I am his Desert Father; he
       is my *gymnasia*,

my Spiritual Exercises

in unnerving—: "HERE BE MONSTERS."

In the night hike up Sinai, I step into the throat
   of the Man of Light.

In darkness, I found St. Catherine's wanting
   light & mounted into stars for it.

In starry dark, cypresses were compasses made
   from shadows night shook waxy dew from—.

In gloom, inspissated walls wrought from stones of legendary fever scale
   stars.

In desert temperatures surrounded,

the monastery candles icons Sinai glows with the gold of, consumed,
   since the 6th century,

in Egyptian firmamental wastes above.

Moses once rose up through them—

& later Elijah
who scoured prophecy from its caves in a lore of fire.

In Sinai, I name radiance of an inner world *mind-in-heart* or *ceaseless prayer.*

In Egypt, I name Mt Sinai *fire-surrounding-iron or clothes-white-as-light*
worn by Moses, Elijah, & XPC.

                "And he brought him forth abroad, and
                said, Look now toward heaven, and tell
                the stars, if thou be able to number
                them."

In aspiring the dark night up the Holy Mtn, an Omophor of clouds
   reposed on my head
diademed with morning star & false dawn.

In prisms its brightness refracted from paradisaical mosaics over an altar
       hewn from

marble & apocalypse.

                          "And there he builded an altar unto the
                          Lord, who appeared unto him."

In the empire of the Man of Light, my life is lapidary with archaeologies,
with the recovery of its sacrificial granites.

In the nocturnal pivot of the Man of Light, my art is an arrhythmical
       aureole,
a hexagram of artisans, a star-map of Sinai, sculpted from sandstone.

In the parched tungsten of the dawn summit, I imagine the mountain a
       cosmic pole & the tablets of emerald transfigured
are Christendom,
an astral crystal dome.

In *Heavens of Light* astronautic monks perplexed with Greek alphabets
       navigate through

                          "as air to the body or flame to the wax
                          body forth syllables for *stars* and *earth*"—:

In my guide, my guided, my Perfect Angel, changing cosmologue into
       evangel,

I trace a slipped tongue:

Arabs baffled *gypt* into *copt*,
& the land became the name of a Christian.

In the hour winey with darkness, we climbed to the top.

In memory of rapt patristic utterances, I revered turrets of lordly boreal
        luster
in leptic moonlight
& night holy & awful.

In holy hour, an Islamic lunula slippers the lynx-eyed confabulon of
        astrology & nocturne—:

In contemplating them, stars are logarithmic oracle Muslims pattern into
        axioms of architecture & prayer both purified of human &
        animal semblance
into a spiritual algebra.

Minarets pierce desert noctuaries
Celestial pens have decorated

                                "God is most great."

                                "Prayer is better than sleep."

In the amplification of the call, birds clatter.

    "We must surely go the way of the stars that shape the divine image."

In the evening before the climb, I felt Sinai in the presence of Islam.

In stepping up onto the switch-back path in darkest hour, I walked in
        Mosaic chronology, reverenced by Jews, Christians, Muslims.

In clearings where camels burble ruminant froth awaiting, bedouins pad
        up & down the mountain night long, leading pilgrims—

in the hour before dawn, chocolate & sweet tea at a kiosk under the
        summit: Qur'ans for sale as well.

In lattices of calligraphy on mosques, on shrines, on tombs, in the valley
      below the mountain,
sands brush configurations of God.

In Jurassic seas of the spirit, Sinai deserts sift aspects of XPC held in
      volumes,
deeply intuited into eremitical instructions &

into icons stacked in Holy Catherine's hallways & corridors. They fume
      with gold force.

In gold air hovering above their Sinai honeyhives, Desert Fathers are
      ætherial
vigils to the poem.

In six-sided lozenges like nave windows amber in evening, sun makes
      lamps of desert sayings

over drones of holy bees:

                                       "You should know no one can hold the
mind by himself."
           —St Gregory of Sinai

                                        "God is the source of every virtue, as sun
is of daylight."
           —St Mark the Ascetic

                                        "Man alone is capable of communion with
God. For to man alone among living crea
tures does God speak—at night through
dreams, by day through the intellect."
           —A Platonist disguised as St Anthony

"You who desire the wondrous Divine
Illumination of our savior IC XPC—who
seek the Divine Fire in your heart—who
desire the candles in you soul to burn
even now—"
                    —Nicephorus the Solitary

"And God reveals His hidden saints so
that some may emulate them & others
have no excuse for not doing so."
                    —St Symeon the New Theologian

"What stars light atop the Holy Mountain,
so Words show me the Body of my Lord."
                    —Orate the Hermit

In the Man of Light, I rose up through Moses Mountain.

In postures recumbent in platinum dawn light, stones of fire incandesce—

in obedient servitude Greek monks through centuries cobbled a staircase
        to the summit of Mt Sinai.

In dawn hour, prayer's been called. They are praying.

                    "Behold their sitting down, and their
                    rising up; *I am their music.*"

In prostrations, Christian pilgrims behold the Burning Bush;

In force, its taproots cleave bedrock under the chapel altar at St Catherine's.
This bush flourishes today
& sends forth shoots

in febrile reach up into columns encrypted with monks' ashes—:

> a terrible arcade
> mirroring Heaven above
> with wishes from its builded hagiography.

In cinders of the sovereign arson of the night sky, Man of Light

reveals himself explosive of effulgence from unoriginate ray
of an atomic hammering of syllables:

In biblical mythemes, mountain mouthes scripture; ceaseless study of
      names eclipses brightness
in Man of Light
in accord with archangelic cabals icons render disturbingly
as ovaline irradiance or the Lord's sad glance.

In the form of eggs, instruction yolky & ephemeral inscribes venerable
      wood.
In overtones retold in Orphic hymns, in Gnostic riddles, in Genesis,
      Word as oviparous glottal.

> "The Holy One created the world like an
> embryo. As the embryo proceeds from
> the navel onwards, so God began to create
> the world from its navel onwards and
> from there it was spread out in different
> directions."

In the dimensions of the monastery,
in the contours of icons, in the split seams, in the chipped enamel,
the basilica reproduces Celestial Jerusalem rooted to the navel of the
      world.

In inner darkness, Man of Light arises & searches his name in the body—:

In Sinai Dark Light, a homologue to "suns" spins my inner pole star, a
   balance constellating energy

in solar logos Man of Light pivots through. I name you *myself*.

In first Light, I name you *horizons upon horizons* & my *supersensory guide*.

In an illustrious early East, I environ the anvil of morning muscling
   warmth—:

In spiritual clarity, Sufi adepts explain to the Man of Light:

> "My image looks at me with my own look;
> I speak to it with its own voice."

In illuminative tallow, their heads aflame—burning bushes of another kind.

> "As highest æthers host no arbors, nor as
> nuvial heights plunge deepest seas, nor as
> pisces lashes through meadows, but as
> wood pulses sanguinous veins, as sap fixes
> stones to fossil splicings, so mind arises in
> body from sinews & blood & godly
> ebullience."

In early hour, Man of Light
mind incandescent
wrists braceleted with zodiacs.

In *Picatrix*, Hermes records the contours of the Man of Light, his hypnotic
   anatomies—:

He writes:

> When I wished to bring to light
> the science of the mystery and modality
> of Creation, I came upon a subterranean vault
> filled with darkness and winds. I saw nothing
> because of the darkness, and behold, a person
> then appeared to me in my sleep in the form of
> the greatest beauty. He said to me: "Take the
> lamp and place it under the glass to shield it from
> the winds; then it will give thee light in spite of
> them. Then go into the underground chamber;
> dig in its center and from there bring forth a cer-
> tain God—made image, designed according to
> the rules of Art. As soon as you have drawn out
> this image, the winds will cease to blow through
> the underground chamber. Then dig in its four
> corners and your will bring to light the knowl-
> edge of the mysteries of Creation, the causes of
> nature, the origins and modalities of things." At
> that I said, "Who then art thou?" He answered:
> "I am they *Perfect Nature.* If thou wish-
> est to see me, call me by my name."

Dawn is resurrection terror.

In configurations of divine light, the letters of the Torah form names,
form names of God,
form appellatives,
form predicates that only suggest the body of the Man of Light.

In dim circulations, the sky is pearly with morning.

In truth I am Byzantine & count hours from a vestigial calendar glorioled

in prayer & frankincense whose girandoles shoot sparks I measure his
       body with.

In Man of Light, I imagine my offering glittering golden. Aspic darkness
       coils the crystal dome
radial stars spur until sunrise. Sunrise is resinous with sap,
piney, miraculous, replete, spreading light on icons of miniature feasts I
       lather with olive oil.

> "Magic and Religion take him up to the
> top of an exceeding high mountain and
> show him, beyond the dark clouds and
> rolling mists at his feet, a vision of the
> celestial city, far off, it may be, but radiant
> with unearthly splendour, bathed in the
> light of dreams."

In the Man of Light, the structure of light is revealed in repetitions of
       reveille,
in summit pilgrimages,
in rock architectonics,
in lion's fire of noon.

In building him up, we show his form.

In descending the Holy Mountain in sunlight, we go out into the world,
       so shapely.

In contemplation of the Man of Light, saintly architects built their
       astronometric patiences
into churches & grounds.

Morning shows St Catherine's bronze then copper, alloyed with light,
wrought at Constantine's wish by Stephanos in 542
who signed each apse, each nave,
each narthex with symbolic objects throughout:
grapes, lambs, pendent icons mark & adore his inhering frame.

In the world, Holy Trinity fifteen centuries later trembles with memories
of the desert, of the steppe, of the pilgrim migration of faith
from the Mediterranean to north of the Black Sea—.

> "Every temple or palace—and, by
> extension, every sacred city or royal
> residence—is a Sacred Mountain, thus
> becoming a center."

Each church in the world emerges as shadow of St Catherine's,

as St Catherine's emerges as shadow of Mt Sinai,
as Mt Sinai is umbral Moses,
concealed within the concealed,
incendiary in radiant oval, one of three dapples in the iris of the Man of
Light.

In hard work bright as the stars, Louis Sullivan's deific edifice is splendid.

It is the Man of Light.

I found light in force:
it phosphoresced its million brilliances.

Following Blake's "No Secrecy in Art!", I offer a few notes of clarification where the poems themselves don't point directly to a source.

Throughout the poems, I make use of three "trigrams" in place of the name of Christ—: XPS & XPI which come from the abbreviations used by calligraphers in the Book of Kells; and xpc, my own conflation of the Kells abbreviation with the "XC IC" that indicates Christ on Orthodox icons. What this means is explained in "Man of Light" on page 97.

Midas
Phrases in italics, including the headpiece and unless otherwise indicated, come from the Arthur Golding translation of *The Metamorphoses*, published in 1567. This would have been the edition Shakespeare used. Marginal citations indicate the source of any quotations that appear on that page of the poem.

Watchfulness
Agios o Theos: "Holy God," invoked at beginning of Divine Liturgy
Hesychia: "Stillness"
Nipsis: "Watchfulness"

St Hesychios the Priest was probably an Abbot monk on Sinai in the 8th or 9th centuries. For fellow monks he composed "On Watchfulness and Holiness," found in *The Philokalia*, eds. G.E.H. Palmer, Philip Sherrard, and Kallistos Ware, Faber & Faber, 1979.

Louis Sullivan, Architect, designed and built Holy Trinity Russian Orthodox Cathedral (now affiliated with the Orthodox Church of America), in Chicago, Illinois, completed in 1902, where it stands today on the corners of W. Haddon St. & N. Leavitt St. in the Ukrainian Village neighborhood where I lived from August 1994 until September 1997, the period during which these poems were written. Properly, its door faces west; clear evenings, it is aflame with setting sun.

St Cyril (Constantine of Thessalonica or Constantine the Priest) lived from 826-869. As well as evangelizing the Slavic lands, he devised an alphabet for the Slavic languages which bears his name. The language as he recorded it remains the liturgical language of the Slavic churches (called Church Slavonic). St Methodius, St Cyril's brother, lived from 815-885. Slavic apostle and enlightener of Eastern Christianity, he also devised the alphabet that bears his brother's name.

Mystic Prayer To The Holy Spirit
St Symeon the New Theologian (949-1022): Born in Asia Minor, he is the best known of the Greek Fathers. Abbot of the monastery at St Mamasin Cappodocia for twenty—five years, he was an 'enthusiastic zealot,' eventually denounced by the patriarch and the holy synod who exiled him to Paloukiton on the Asiatic coast of the Bosphorus, where he died thirteen years later. Mine is a version from a French translation from the Greek.

Man of Light
Quotations, in order, can be found in the following sources:
The Zohar (4); *Genesis 15:5*; *Genesis 12:7*; Henry Corbin, *The Man of Light in Iranian Sufism*; Alfred Guillaume, *Islam* (2); *The Man of Light*; *The Philokalia* (6); *Lamentations*; Mircea Eliade, *The Myth of the Eternal Return*; *The Man of Light*; Lucretius, *De Rerum Natura*; *The Man of Light*; Sir James Frazer, *The Golden Bough*; *The Myth of the Eternal Return*.

Among the treasures kept at St Catherine's monastery, one finds icons dating back to the 6th Century, one of the only places in the world with icons so old, due to the fact that St Catherine's was too far away to have had its icons smashed during the Iconoclast controversy; and one also finds the Burning Bush, full, green, and dangling in the monastery courtyard, supposedly the only place in the world where this bush will grow (attempts have been made to foster shoots elsewhere).

Peter O'Leary has edited two volumes of Ronald Johnson's poetry—*To Do As Adam Did: Selected Poems* (Talisman House) and *The Shrubberies* (Flood Editions)—and is the author of *Gnostic Contagion: Robert Duncan & the Poetry of Illness*, forthcoming from Wesleyan University Press. He lives in St. Louis with his wife & son.